JEFFERS COUNTRY

JEFFERS COUNTRY

THE SEED PLOTS OF
ROBINSON JEFFERS' POETRY

poetry by Robinson Jeffers

photographs by Horace Lyon

Scrimshaw Press 1971

"Ocean" and the selections from *Cawdor* are copyright 1928
by Robinson Jeffers and are reprinted by permission of New
Directions Publishing Company. For the remainder of Jeffers'
poetry and for copyrighted material from *The Selected Poetry
of Robinson Jeffers*, acknowledgement is made to Random House,
Inc. The introductions by Robinson and Una Jeffers are
reprinted through the kind permission of Donnan Jeffers.

The Scrimshaw Press / 149 Ninth Street / San Francisco 94103

Publisher's Foreword

This book has lived a shadowy half-life in the thirty-five years since its conception. Late in 1935, Horace and Edna Lyon were struck with the thought that admirers of Robinson Jeffers' verse — and there were many — would have an enhanced appreciation of his work if they could see images of the country in which so much of it centered, that immense broken California coastline south from Carmel through Big Sur. After some experimenting, the Lyons knew that they had the beginnings of at least a booklet, "Jeffers Country," and they showed the first photographs to Una Jeffers. She was an energetic supporter of her husband's work and began to encourage the Lyons in every way — suggesting and identifying locations, making selections of his poetry and doing all she could to achieve an authentic wedding of photograph to poem. Jeffers himself could hardly have been more indifferent to self-promotion, but he too was drawn in, to write identifications on the backs of pictures and to keep some of them with him as he wrote new poetry. A close friendship formed and the Jeffers and the Lyons began to hope (with the poet's slowly warming agreement) that a book might come from this combination of words and images.

For all of his personal separateness, Jeffers kindled extremely loyal sentiments in his readers in those years and if those readers were relatively few in number — the normal state of things in American arts — his critical successes so interested an editor at the new pictorial weekly, *Life*, that they laid plans for a selection of Jeffers' poetry and Lyon's photographs in an "Americana" issue in June of 1938. That project languished, but in the meanwhile, one of Jeffers' friends, Ted Lilienthal, was drawing up impressive plans for the book which everyone dreamed of, to be printed in San Francisco by the Grabhorns in huge format, with Lyon's original prints tipped-in by hand. This plan also came to nothing (not without reason), but you do see in our *Jeffers Country* both of the introductions written for the earlier project. There were subsequent flurries of interest in the manuscript and the photographs have themselves been widely used to illustrate Jeffers country on other occasions — the most notable one being that which marked the opening of the poetry section of the Library of Congress early in 1941. At that time, Una Jeffers wrote to the Lyons:

> "If your daughter hasn't been to the Library of Congress tell her to go at once for her father's sake! There are, I think, 12 *long* cases of Jeffers' exhibit & 2 of them are devoted to your Carmel prints. *Every one* you gave me is on display — properly spaced & with the captions printed on separate cards, beside them. The effect of the whole set is magnificent. Also the Grabhorn trial proof sheets are up . . . Robin had a regular triumph in Washington. The hall was filled, then they put people in an adjoining hall — where he could be heard but not seen. They turned away several hundred. . . ."

Publishing is a chancy business, and it is easy to understand why this book has been so long a-borning. The tradition in reproducing fine landscape photography has been that it be massive, total, definitive. Horace Lyon has never claimed any of these adjectives for his own pictures, and we are presenting them as he intended them — as faithful servants of the verse, a unique relationship to the very sources of Jeffers' vision. The poetry itself (Jeffers died in 1962) has been relatively inaccessible for some time though there is a recent paperback selection available. We have done our utmost to respect his positioning of the words on the page and we have, with one exception, kept the verse in our book in the same chronological order in which it was written.

Many friends have helped to bring this book about. We are grateful to Donnan Jeffers for his full cooperation and his permission to print his parents' introductions. We are delighted that William Everson and Peter Bartlett conspired to bring this project to our attention. But, most important, Horace and Edna Lyon and their son, Peter, have been such stalwarts, so involved in developing the basic plan for this book that we can truly say that its virtues are all theirs.

So, then, we are pleased indeed to honor the original collaboration of the poet with his friend. Here is your guide to the edge of another country, a mythical landscape grown from living earth: Jeffers Country.

Frederick Mitchell

Robinson Jeffers:

Horace Lyon told us that some of his friends had asked him, when he revisited the east after coming to live in Carmel, whether there was any such country as pictured in Jeffers' verses, or was it mere fantasy? He had assured them that it was as real as New Jersey and still they seemed skeptical; easterners are bound to think of orange groves when you speak of California; so he was going to take some photographs and show them. Perhaps he would make a little book of the photographs: if so, might he call it "Jeffers Country"? Certainly, I said, if he wanted to. I ought to have thought of the people who really have names on this coast, because they have lived their lives in it, and their fathers before them; whilst I have only sat in its doorway and written verses about it. But the photographs meant very little to me, until I saw them.

Once seen, they stirred me to delight and enthusiasm, and sharp recognition; as in that story about Milton's daughter, when several portraits of her father were shown her and she chose one of them: "This is the very man, this is my father!" So I felt about these photographs, looking at them successively: "This is the very coast that I love, the forms and the moods, and something of the life." While I was still enjoying the pictures another thought brushed my mind. I thought of the cant we have heard about art — cant that no one has to believe in, but it seems to be generally voiced, if not accepted — that art must not be representational; it should not, if that were possible, even suggest nature; it should reject nature and produce its own forms, follow its own laws. For a moment I felt meanly suspicious: is it possible that *photography* has driven the doctrinaires into this sterile corner? Then I remembered that the same cant is recited about other arts than painting; and that even photographers have sometimes been influenced by it, so far as the honest lens would allow them. While all the while it is obvious . . .

I dropped the thought unfinished, preferring to look through the pictures again, recognizing each scene, refreshing the emotion it had brought me, often remembering the insufficient verses through which I had tried to express the emotion. That is one reason for writing narrative poetry, and in this case a principal one: because certain scenes awake an emotion that seems to overflow the limits of lyric or description, one tries to express it in terms of human lives. Thus each of my too many stories has grown up like a plant from some particular canyon or promontory, some particular relationship of rock and water, wood, grass and mountain. Here were photographs of their seed-plots.

I thought, "Whether the plants are good is beyond my knowledge, but certainly the garden is" and the incidents of our first acquaintance with it came vividly to my mind. It was in December 1914, just after the world began its violent change. In those days one did not attempt the coast-road by motor; we

waited in the dawn twilight for the horse-drawn mail stage that drove twice a week to Big Sur, where the road ended then; and it was night before we arrived, and every mile of the forty had been enchanted. We, and our dog, were the only passengers on the mail stage; we were young and in love, perhaps that contributed to the enchantment. And the coast had displayed all its winter magic for us: drifts of silver rain through great gorges, clouds dragging on the summits, storm on the rock shore, sacred calm under the redwoods.

There had already been strong storms that winter, and at Soberanes Creek the cypress trees around the farmhouse were blown to pieces. Sea-lions roared on the Lobos Rocks off shore, while the man of the house told us that last night his hundred-pound grindstone, which he kept by the back door, had been blown a-round the house to the front steps; here it lay. At Notley's Landing we saw the ruinous old lumber-mill (which blew down this present year, after having stood for so many) and heard the story about it. In the gorge of Mill Creek we passed under a rusted cable sagging to a stuck skip, and we were told about the lime-kilns up the canyon, cold and forgotten, with the forest growing over them. Here we changed horses, near a lonely farmhouse where an eighty-year-old man lay dying; he was dying hard, he had been dying for a week. There were forty bee-hives in rows in front of his house. On a magnificent hillside opposite a mountain-peak stood a comparatively prosperous farmhouse, apple trees behind it, and the man who lived there had killed his father with rat-poison and married his step-mother. This was the "still small music of humanity" that we heard among the mountains; there were only five or six inhabitants in forty miles, but each one had a story. We passed the little hand-hewn cabin that a man had built twenty years before and then gone up to San Francisco and been shanghaied; at last escaping the sea he came back and died here, and lay undiscovered for a month. In the cloud on top of Sur Hill a bearded old hermit met the stage, to take delivery of a pilot-biscuit he had sent for. Pilot-biscuit! He had not a tooth in his head. Farther, we drove along a steep above oaks and sycamores: this was the place where a wagon loaded with drowned bodies from a shipwreck had tipped over: the bodies rolled down the slope, and it was never known whether all were gathered up again. We came down to the Sur River, and passed the albino redwood that still grows there, shining in the forest darkness, shoots of snow-

white foliage growing from the stump of a lightning-struck tree: not a human story, but strange enough to be. At last we came to the farm at the end of the road, where we spent the night in a little cabin under immense redwoods. Our dog lay at the bed-foot and snarled all night long, terrified by the noises of water and the forest odors.

This was the journey by horse stage. Twenty years later we sailed over these mountains in a cabin plane, ten thousand feet above their highest, and it pleased me to see that even by this test the coast was not tamed nor flattened. The ocean looked more beautiful than from below, spread like a peacock's tail, shining all its colors; the mountains were simply not changed, dark, fierce, massive, and as wild as the back of a grizzly bear.   *Robinson Jeffers, 1938*

Una Jeffers:

Looking southward from our headland we see beyond the mouth of the Carmel River the gentle rounded outlines of the Santa Lucia Mountains, bright green with pasture and dark with thickets of chaparral and sage. One yellowed ivory scar marks the quarry where, long ago, Indians hewed out blocks of chalkstone to build the Spanish mission church, San Carlos del Rio Carmelo. The mountains look serenely lovely, with no hint of the magnificent and menacing face they turn toward the sea. This range, narrow but rising in double or triple ridges, stretches southward along the coast for a hundred miles.

The river too is quiet, except when winter floods rage down the valley to battle the waves across the sand-bar, or surge out in a tremendous bore through new-cut channels. At most times it spreads out like a placid lake, and trickles into the adjoining water-meadows. Here among reeds and tough grasses the pools reflect every changing hue of sky and clouds, and the shadow of the hills lies darkly. The air is full of bird-songs, and the plop-plop of game birds that rest in their flights and feed here — ducks and geese and wild swans, with the local herons and passing egrets — every day a different group. But a myriad of gulls are constant on the sand-spits by the open water. They fish and swirl on flashing white wings; sometimes, before storm, they float high aloft for hours, weaving great complicated circles in some precise ritual. Unwieldy pelicans feed here too, and row away to their sea-rocks on heavy wings.

The coast-road, the great San Simeon Highway, crosses the river just beyond the Mission. It was completed in 1937, a hundred miles of road; its construction consumed seventeen years of labor and eight million dollars, indicative of the difficult terrain. Beyond, no longer gentle now, the mountains hurry to the sea in great precipices, slashed by canyons, only seldom flattening to a few acres of possible plowland. Cattle, pasturing for centuries where they could, have left the welts of their hoof-tracks criss-crossing many a steep hillside. Canyons, gushing springs and streams, are thickly wooded with redwoods and pines, laurels, tan-oaks, maples and sycamores, and, high up, the rosy-barked madrones. Near the Little Sur River there are dunes, whose drifting sands defy any boundaries of the road. Beyond, the Point Sur lighthouse sits atop a rock like St. Michael's Mount off Cornwall. From three hundred and fifty feet above the sea the powerful lens and bellowing siren warn mariners that many a stout ship has broken up along this terrible shore, which mile after mile is jagged with sharp cliffs and narrow inlets with only an occasional furlong of white-sanded beach, inaccessible from above. Lashing waves roll in, incredibly green and blue beyond the foam, menacing and gray in storm. Color, *color* on land and sea, greens and tawny yellows, and the millefleurs tapestry.

Name the flowers to conjure up the colors — blues of wild lilac and lupin, lark-spur and iris and blue-eyed grass; gold of poppies and yarrow and the yellow lupin, wild pansies and wall-flowers; and white heather, white wild lilac, candle-white yucca, and sometimes snow-on-the-mountain. Flashing bird-wings too, red-winged blackbirds and golden finches, blue jays and hummingbirds, darting red and emerald. And high above, arrogant hawks hover, marsh hawks and sparrow hawks, redtails and peregrine falcons. Vultures too peering down, and a rare pair of eagles. Even on sunny days there will be a vagrant wisp of luminous fog creeping like a live thing in and out the canyons.

Long ago I read in Dorothy Wordsworth's *Journal* an observation of hers in some remote Highland glen. She was "conscious of the interest man gives to nature, and still more, the dignity nature gives to man." They enhance each other; we have realized their interplay as we have walked and ridden over this coast land, meditating on remote farmhouses, evidences of formerly vigorous and self-sustained life. Only a heart of horn could fail to quicken to the mute tokens around a deserted farm, old cart wheels and antique gear, faded calico rags, a caved-in well, clumps of ragged geranium and the startling clarity of calla lilies. Never unkempt, however long lost, these cold flowers rise on high stems out of shining leaves. And the many abandoned enterprises: old saw-mills, the tottering buildings at Notley's Landing, where once great loads of redwood and tan-bark went out on ships; the coal mine up Mal Paso, where only a hump hidden by thistles indicates the slide that covered its mouth and twenty Chinese workmen as well. Other random diggings too, where men have  vainly sought the lost gold mine of the Padres; or sought the loot buried by the bandits, Vásquez and Murrieta.

Up Mill Creek was the most extensive of the old enterprises, lime-kilns, whose output slid on skips down to the sea on a steel cable slung high above the canyon. No road goes to the kilns, only a broken trail crossing and re-crossing a tumbling stream, whose fords were washed away long ago. A traveller treads precariously across on broken tree-trunks, or leaps from the tall white kilns smothered with vines and poison oak. Redwoods pushed through the walls and tilted the floors of the house, empty save for a broken bench or table, or a rusty iron stove. In one house the portrait of an old lady startled us. It was one of those old-fashioned crayon enlargements common enough in the nineties, framed heavily in machine-carved wood with metal embellishments. From her position on the floor, propped against a sagging door, the old lady looked at us with prim and steadfast eyes. Her sensitive mouth and neat garb were curiously arresting in that situation. Afterwards we often speculated about her plight, and sensed the forest growth closing in, the wild creatures brushing against her. Years went by. Once more we journeyed to the kilns, and Horace Lyon with us. The lady awaited our coming. We lifted her to a broken window, and Horace photographed her there. On an impulse I sent the picture with a note to *Time*, which published it with the caption "Santa Lucia Lady — who is she?" Other people found her interesting, too, for I received letters about her from all over the country, and at last one from an old lady in Ohio, identifying this picture of her mother and explaining its mysterious abandonment.

Horace Lyon caught the atmosphere at the kilns, as he has of many places in this region, toward which he seems to have a peculiarly sympathetic relationship. No other person, either with lens or paints, has approached his understanding of its drama and stark terror and beauty. If ill luck ever pushed us from this place of our choice, Robin and I would certainly carry away with us, among our best treasures, this series of Horace Lyon's photographs of "Jeffers Country."   *Una Jeffers, 1938*

JEFFERS COUNTRY

BIRDS

The fierce musical cries of a couple of sparrowhawks hunting
    on the headland,
Hovering and darting, their heads northwestward,
Prick like silver arrows shot through a curtain the noise of the
    ocean
Trampling its granite; their red backs gleam
Under my window around the stone corners; nothing gracefuller,
    nothing
Nimbler in the wind. Westward the wave-gleaners,
The old gray sea-going gulls are gathered together, the north-
    west wind wakening
Their wings to the wild spirals of the wind-dance.
Fresh as the air, salt as the foam, play birds in the bright wind,
    fly falcons
Forgetting the oak and the pinewood, come gulls
From the Carmel sands and the sands at the river-mouth, from
    Lobos and out of the limitless
Power of the mass of the sea, for a poem
Needs multitude, multitudes of thoughts, all fierce, all flesh-eaters,
    musically clamorous
Bright hawks that hover and dart headlong, and ungainly
Gray hunters fledged with desire of transgression, salt slimed
    beaks, from the sharp
Rock-shores of the world and the secret waters.

from THE WOMEN AT POINT SUR

Onorio Vasquez,
Young seer of visions who lives with his six brothers
On the breast of Palo Corona mountain looking north-
    ward,
Watches his brother Vidal and Julio the youngest
Play with a hawk they shot from the mountain cloud,
The wing broken. They crucified the creature,
A nail in the broken wing on the barn wall
Between the pink splinters of bone and a nail in the
    other.

from THE WOMEN AT POINT SUR

In the morning
The inexhaustible clouds flying up from the south
Stream rain, the gullies of the hills grow alive, the
    creeks flood, the summer sand-bars
Burst from their mouths, from every sea-mouth wedges
    of yellow, yellow tongues.

from THE WOMEN AT POINT SUR

He brushed his clothing at dawn,
And washed when he found water. At a prosperous
    farmhouse
Lodging was refused him, he went on southward
And saw from the road over the great bronze height
Eastward the mountain Pico Blanco, westward the rock
    at Point Sur crowned with its lighthouse
Against great waters; a gated way dropped seaward,
He followed, he came to the gaunt farmhouse that stood
High over gap-roofed barns and broken wagons;
They had told him he might be given lodging at Mor-
    head's
High cube-shaped house, redwood logs squared and
    jointed,
Blackened with ancient weathers, chinked with white
    plaster,
Striped like a zebra with the white plaster, and the
    porch
Rotting under its rose-vine.

from THE WOMEN AT POINT SUR

"You choose to ignore consciousness, incredible how
    quickly
The American mind short-circuits by ignoring its object.
Something in the gelded air of the country. Tell Mrs.
    Barclay,
No need of writing, if she pleases may follow me.
Do you know whether my daughter's with her, a girl
Twenty years old? Oh, you'd have noticed.
I shall have to do something, God thinks through action
And all this show is God's brain, the water, the cloud
    yonder,
The coast hills, thinking the thing out to conclusion.
Tell her that I'm walking southward."

from THE WOMEN AT POINT SUR

They left the buck-eyes,
And over a ridge of crumbled earth and dead grass
To a dry stream-bed stubbed with dwarf oaks. She
    halting
In the yellow pit that winter cataracts had sunk,
Hard green dry leaves shielded.

from THE WOMEN AT POINT SUR

The fog-bank that all day far off had lain slant
On the sea northward, perhaps indeed had drawn in-
    land
And covered the shore like a flood and climbed up the
    hill-slope.
Though the sun blazed there came a ground-fog; and the
    wind
Was like the draught from a cellar, from the low sea
Sharp with its odors.

from CAWDOR

"Now's the other fool's turn
To speak: it makes me mad to have to spread out my
     foolishness.
I never had time to play with colored ribbons, I was
     brought up hard. I did a man's work at twelve
And bossed a gang at eighteen. That gets you nowhere. I
     learned that ruling poor men's hands is nothing,
Ruling men's money's a wedge in the world. But after I'd
     split it open a crack I looked in and saw
The trick inside it, the filthy nothing, the fooled and rot-
     ten faces of rich and successful men.
And the sons they have. Then I came down from the city.
I saw this place and got it. I was what you call honest
     but I was hard; the little Mexican
Cried when I got it. A canyon full of redwoods and hills
     guaranteed not to contain gold."

from CAWDOR

"But see," she looked from the ocean
sundown to the violet hills and the great moon,
"Because I choose to be safe all this grows hateful. What
shall I do?" He said scornfully: "Like others,
Take what you dare and let the rest go." "That is no
limit. I dare," she answered. He looked aside
At the dark presence of the ocean moving its foam secretly
below the red west, and thought
"Well, what does she want?" "Nothing," she said as if she
had heard him. "But I wish to God
I were the hunter." She went up to the house,
And there for days was silent as a sheathed knife,
Attending her sick father and ruling the housework
With bitter eyes. At night she endured Cawdor if he
pleased
As this earth endures man.

from CAWDOR

                In the afternoon the wind
Fell, and the spray in the wind waxed into rain.
The men came home, they boarded the broken window.
The rain increased all night. At dawn a high sea-bird,
If any had risen so high, watching the hoary light
Creep down to the sea, under the cloud-streams, down
The many canyons the great sea-wall of coast
Is notched with like a murderer's gun-stock, would have
        seen
Each canyon's creek-mouth smoke its mud-brown torrent
Into the shoring gray; and as the light gained
Have seen the whole wall gleam with a glaze of water.

from CAWDOR

In the bright of dawn, before sunrise began,
The lank steers wheeled their line when he waved his arms.
He cursed them with obscene words . . . but why? . . . and
    there stood
Thirty in a row, all in a row like soldiers
Staring at him with strained-up heads. He was in the
    pasture
On the highest dome of the hill.
Wild fragrant wind blew from the burning east,
A handful of cloud high up in the air caught fire and
    vanished.
A point of more excessive light appeared
On the ridge by the lone oak and enlarged.
Without doubt, the sun. But if it were the horn of a
    flaming beast:
We'd have a horned beast to see by.

TOR HOUSE

If you should look for this place after a handful of lifetimes:
Perhaps of my planted forest a few
May stand yet, dark-leaved Australians or the coast cypress, haggard
With storm-drift; but fire and the axe are devils.
Look for foundations of sea-worn granite, my fingers had the art
To make stone love stone, you will find some remnant.
But if you should look in your idleness after ten thousand years:
It is the granite knoll on the granite
And lava tongue in the midst of the bay, by the mouth of the Carmel
River-valley, these four will remain
In the change of names. You will know it by the wild sea-fragrance of wind
Though the ocean may have climbed or retired a little;
You will know it by the valley inland that our sun and our moon were born from
Before the poles changed; and Orion in December
Evenings was strung in the throat of the valley like a lamp-lighted bridge.
Come in the morning you will see white gulls
Weaving a dance over blue water, the wane of the moon
Their dance-companion, a ghost walking
By daylight, but wider and whiter than any bird in the world.
My ghost you needn't look for; it is probably
Here, but a dark one, deep in the granite, not dancing on wind
With the mad wings and the day moon.

39

OCEAN

It dreams in the deepest sleep, it remembers the storm
    last month or it feels the far storm
Off Unalaska and the lash of the sea-rain.
It is never mournful but wise, and takes the magical
    misrule of the steep world
With strong tolerance, its depth is not moved
From where the green sun fails to where the thin red clay
    lies on the basalt
And there has never been light nor life.
The black crystal, the untroubled fountain, the roots of
    endurance.

        Therefore I belted
The house and the tower and courtyard with stone,
And have planted the naked foreland with future forest
    toward noon and morning: for it told me,
The time I was gazing in the black crystal,
To be faithful in storm, patient of fools, tolerant of
    memories and the muttering prophets,
It is needful to have night in one's body.

from THE LOVING SHEPHERDESS

         Clare travelled northward, and sometimes
Half running, more often loitering, and the sheep fed.
In the afternoon she led them into the willows,
And choosing a green pool of the shallow stream
Bathed, while the sheep bleated to her from the shoals.
They made a pleasant picture, the girl and her friends, in the
     green shade
Shafted with golden light falling through the alder branches.
     Her body, the scarecrow garments laid by,
Though hermit-ribbed and with boyishly flattened flanks hardly
     a woman's,
Was smooth and flowing, glazed with bright water, the shoulders
     and breasts beautiful, and moved with a rapid confidence
That contradicted her mind's abstractions.

from THE LOVING SHEPHERDESS

He said gravely
"There's hardly a man on the coast wouldn't have helped you
Except in that house. There, I think they *need* help.
Well, come and we'll live the night." "How far?" she sighed
Faintly, and he said "Our place is away up-canyon,
You'll find it stiff traveling by daylight even.
To-night's a camp."

He led her to the bridge, and there
Found dry sticks up the bank, leavings of an old flood, under
    the spring of the timbers,
And made a fire against the creekside under the road for a roof.
    He stripped her of the dripping cloak
And clothed her in his, the oil-skin had kept it dry, and spread her
    the blanket from under his saddle to lie on.
The bridge with the tarred road-bed on it was a roof
Over their heads; the sheep, when Clare commanded them, lay
    down like dogs by the fire. The horse was tethered
To a clump of willow in the night outside.

44

from THE LOVING SHEPHERDESS

                              "Come, Clare.
The place is pleasant and alone, up the deep canyon, beside the
    old quarry and the kilns where they burnt the lime.
A hundred laborers used to live there, but now the woods have
    grown back, the cabins are standing empty,
The roads are gone. I think the old masonry kilns are beautiful,
    standing like towers in the deep forest,
But cracked and leaning, and maidenhair fern grows from the
    cracks. The creek makes music below. Come, Clare.
It is deep with peace. When I have to go about and work on
    men's farms for wages I long for that place
Like some one thinking of water in deserts. Sometimes we hear
    the sea's thunder, far down the deep gorge.
The darkness under the trees in spring is starry with flowers,
    with redwood sorrel, colt's foot, wakerobin,
The slender-stemmed pale yellow violets,
And Solomon's seal that makes intense islands of fragrance in
    April."

from THE LOVING SHEPHERDESS

        Clare Walker had crossed the ridge and
  gone down
To the mouth of Cawdor's Canyon. Japanese tenants
Now kept the house; short broad-faced men who planted
Lettuces in the garden against the creek-side
And beans on the hill. The barns were vacant, the cattle
Were vanished from the high pastures. The men were friendly,
Clare begged at their hands a little oil to soften
The bandage on Leader's wound; she'd torn her spent dress
In strips to bind it, and went now without clothing
But the long brown cloak.

from THE LOVING SHEPHERDESS

          She went northward, and on a foreland
Found vacant cabins around a ruined saw-mill;
And finding sacks of dry straw with a worn blanket
In one of the cabins, slept well and awoke refreshed
To travel on slowly northward in the glad sunlight
And sparkle of the sea. But the next day was dark,
And one of the wethers died, she never knew why,
She wept and went on.

from THURSO'S LANDING

"We may help out the beasts, but a man mustn't be beaten.
That was a little too easy, to pop himself off because he went
    broke.
I was ten years old, I tried not to despise the soft stuff
That ran away to the dark from a touch of trouble:
Because the lime-kilns failed and the lumber mill
Ran out of redwood.
My mother took up his ruins and made a farm;
She wouldn't run away, to death or charity. Mark and I helped.
We lost most of the land but we saved enough."
"Think of one man owning so many canyons:
Sovranes, Granite," she counted on her fingers, "Garapatas, Palo
    Colorado,
Rocky Creek, and this Mill Creek." "Oh, that was nothing, the
    land was worth nothing
In those days, only for lime and redwood."

from THURSO'S LANDING

"You'd think
This rocked-in gorge would be the last place in the world to bear
    the brunt: but it's not so: they told me
This is the prow and plunging cutwater,
This rock shore here, bound to strike first, and the world behind
    will watch us endure prophetical things
And learn its fate from our ends."

from THURSO'S LANDING

             Suddenly emerging at the creek-mouth beach
      they breathed and stood still. The narrow crescent
Of dark gravel, sundered away from the world by its walls of
      cliff, smoked in a burst of sun
And murmured in the high tide through its polished pebbles. The
      surf broke dazzling on fins of rock far out,
And foam flowed on the ankles of the precipice. Helen looked
      up, cliff over cliff, the great naked hill
All of one rifted rock covering the northwest sky; and said: "It's
      called Thurso's Landing. That's something,
To have the standing sea-cliffs named after you. His father used
      to swing down the barrels of lime
From the head of that to the hulls of ships. The old wrecks of
      rusting engines are still to be seen up there,
And the great concrete block that anchors the cable."

from GIVE YOUR HEART TO THE HAWKS

They met at Frasers'

And crossed the ridge; and were picketing the horses
Where they could ride no farther, on the airy brink
Above the great slides of the thousand-foot cliff.
They were very gay, colorful mites on the edge of the world.
    The men divided the pack to carry;
Lance Fraser, being strongest, took most.

Far down below, the

    broad ocean burned like a vast cat's eye
Pupilled by the track of sun; but eastward, beyond the white-
    grassed hump of the ridge, the day moon stood bleak
And badly shaped, face of stained clay, above the limestone fang
    of one of the Ventana mountains
Just its own color.

from A LITTLE SCRAPING

This mountain sea-coast is real,
For it reaches out far into past and future;
It is part of the great and timeless excellence of things. A few
Lean cows drift high up the bronze hill;
The heavy-necked plow-team furrows the foreland, gulls tread
    the furrow;
Time ebbs and flows but the rock remains.
Two riders of tired horses canter on the cloudy ridge;
Topaz-eyed hawks have the white air;
Or a woman with jade-pale eyes, hiding a knife in her hand,
Goes through cold rain over gray grass.

STILL THE MIND SMILES

Still the mind smiles at its own rebellions,
Knowing all the while that civilization and the other evils
That make humanity ridiculous, remain
Beautiful in the whole fabric, excesses that balance each other
Like the paired wings of a flying bird.
Misery and riches, civilization and squalid savagery,
Mass war and the odor of unmanly peace:
Tragic flourishes above and below the normal of life.
In order to value this fretful time
It is necessary to remember our norm, the unaltered passions,
The same-colored wings of imagination,
That the crowd clips, in lonely places new-grown; the unchanged
Lives of herdsmen and mountain farms,
Where men are few, and few tools, a few weapons, and their
    dawns are beautiful.
From here for normal one sees both ways,
And listens to the splendor of God, the exact poet, the sonorous
Antistrophe of desolation to the strophe multitude.

from SUBJECTED EARTH

                        I remembered impatiently
How the long bronze mountain of my own coast,
Where color is no account and pathos ridiculous, the sculpture
      is all,
Breaks the arrows of the setting sun
Over the enormous mounded eyeball of ocean.

RETURN

A little too abstract, a little too wise,
It is time for us to kiss the earth again,
It is time to let the leaves rain from the skies,
Let the rich life run to the roots again.
I will go down to the lovely Sur Rivers
And dip my arms in them up to the shoulders.
I will find my accounting where the alder leaf quivers
In the ocean wind over the river boulders.
I will touch things and things and no more thoughts,
That breed like mouthless May-flies darkening the sky,
The insect clouds that blind our passionate hawks
So that they cannot strike, hardly can fly.
Things are the hawk's food and noble is the mountain, Oh noble
Pico Blanco, steep sea-wave of marble.

from STEELHEAD

                              Toward the canyon sea-mouth
The water spread wide and shoal, fingering through many chan-
    nels down a broad flood-bed, and a mob of sea-gulls
Screamed at each other.

from SUCH COUNSELS YOU GAVE TO ME

                    They tied their horses at one of those
      cairns of rock
That stand along the ridges like kings' graves. Ernie stayed
      by to watch them,
And he lent France his gun. She and Paul went down
Over the verge of the height and heard the fire's roar
Devour the wind's. They hurried and stood at their
      vantages, north and south
The glen-head where brush grew highest; half way down
      a few trees
Stood terribly distinct against the fire-curtain.

from THE COAST-ROAD

A horseman high alone as an eagle on the spur of the mountain
    over Mirmas Canyon draws rein, looks down
At the bridge-builders, men, trucks, the power-shovels, the teem-
    ing end of the new coast-road at the mountain's base.
He sees the loops of the road go northward, headland beyond
    headland, into gray mist over Fraser's Point,
He shakes his fist and makes the gesture of wringing a chicken's
    neck, scowls and rides higher.

THE BEAKS OF EAGLES

An eagle's nest on the head of an old redwood on one of the
    precipice-footed ridges
Above Ventana Creek, that jagged country which nothing but a
    falling meteor will ever plow; no horseman
Will ever ride there, no hunter cross this ridge but the winged
    ones, no one will steal the eggs from this fortress.
The she-eagle is old, her mate was shot long ago, she is now mated
    with a son of hers.
When lightning blasted her nest she built it again on the same
    tree, in the splinters of the thunderbolt.
The she-eagle is older than I; she was here when the fires of
    eighty-five raged on these ridges,
She was lately fledged and dared not hunt ahead of them but ate
    scorched meat. The world has changed in her time;
Humanity has multiplied, but not here; men's hopes and thoughts
    and customs have changed, their powers are enlarged,
Their powers and their follies have become fantastic,
The unstable animal never has been changed so rapidly. The
    motor and the plane and the great war have gone over him,
And Lenin has lived and Jehovah died: while the mother-eagle
Hunts her same hills, crying the same beautiful and lonely cry and
    is never tired; dreams the same dreams,
And hears at night the rock-slides rattle and thunder in the throats
    of these living mountains.
                        It is good for man
To try all changes, progress and corruption, powers, peace and
    anguish, not to go down the dinosaur's way
Until all his capacities have been explored: and it is good for him
To know that his needs and nature are no more changed in fact
    in ten thousand years than the beaks of eagles.

Contents

Herewith a listing of the Jeffers poetry and the Lyon photographs in this book. The photographs are identified by Lyon's own titles and appear in italics. The poems' titles appear in quotation marks and are followed by a reference to the volume and page where the poem may be found. *SP = The Selected Poetry of Robinson Jeffers. WPS = The Women at Point Sur. Caw = Cawdor. SC = Such Counsels You Gave to Me.*

Contents   77

Type for this
book was set at the
Cranium Press, San Fran-
cisco, in linotype Aldus and handset
Palatino. Cal-Central Press, Sacramento,
printed 4000 copies by offset lithography on
Champion Carnival Offset. 3500 were softbound
and 500 casebound by Cardoza-James. The work
was completed in October, 1971, with spec-
ial thanks due Clifford Burke, Rudy
Petschek, Richard Schuettge
and Mary Robertson.
Frederick Mitchell
designed it